HEART TO HEART

Praying with the Saints

Compiled by
Patricia Mitchell

the WORD
among us

The Word Among Us Press

9639 Doctor Perry Road

Ijamsville, Maryland 21754

ISBN: 0-932085-49-0

Cover design by David Crosson

Made and printed in the United States of America.

Contents

Introduction

And Jesus told them a parable, to the effect that they ought always to pray and not lose heart. (Luke 18:1)

Jesus' parable portrayed the persistent widow who would not let the unrighteous judge ignore justice. She was successful simply because she did not give up. "And will not God vindicate his elect, who cry to him day and night?" (Luke 18:7), Jesus asked. The story is an invitation for all of us to cry out to the Lord with great hope that he will always hear our prayers.

Whether we pray in our own words or with words written by others, God is always eager to reveal his face and to impart his love, wisdom, and grace. We may pray in thanksgiving for our blessings or cry out in distress because of our trials. Whatever the reason, when we open our hearts to God, he never turns us away. He knows what we need, even before we do.

The saints were persistent in prayer simply because they loved God with all their hearts and were keenly aware of their absolute need for him. Our rich Catholic tradition has provided us with saints who are our role models and guides. By praying the prayers that they wrote, we can adopt their own disposition before God of love, humility, praise, trust, and thanksgiving.

Some of the prayers in this book are well known; others you may discover for the first time. In every case, the prayer was selected because it eloquently expressed some attitude of the heart that is essential to anyone who desires a closer walk with the Lord. We can use these prayers as "starters" for our own prayer and praise to God. They can help to focus us as we begin to pray and to draw us into a deeper intimacy with the Lord. They may even inspire us to write our own special prayers! (If a prayer arouses your interest in a specific saint, turn to the index in the back of the book, where there is a brief summary on each saint.)

"Let my prayer be counted as incense before thee,

and the lifting up of my hands as an evening sacrifice!"
(Psalm 141:2) Our prayers truly are a fragrance to the
Lord, who is pleased whenever we lift up our hearts and
minds to him. May the parable of the persistent widow
encourage us to ask Jesus for all the gifts we need to
become his disciples. Above all, let us ask the Father
to pour out his Holy Spirit upon us, so that we may sing
his praises all the days of our lives.

The Word Among Us Press

O Consuming Fire!

Prayer to the Holy Face of Jesus

St. Thérèse of Lisieux

O adorable Face of Jesus,
Sole beauty which ravishes my heart,
Vouchsafe to impress on my soul your Divine Likeness,
so that it may not be possible for you
to look at your spouse without beholding yourself.

O my Beloved, for love of you I am content not to see
here on earth the sweetness of your glance,
nor to feel the ineffable kiss of your sacred lips,
but I beg of you to inflame me with your love,
so that it may consume me quickly
and that soon I may behold
your glorious Face in heaven.

Let Me Hold Fast to You

St. Bernard of Clairvaux

Let me hold fast to you, beautiful Lord,
whom the angels themselves yearn to look upon.
Wherever you go, I will follow you.
If you pass through fire, I will not flinch,
I fear no evil when you are with me.
You carry my griefs, because you grieve for my sake.
You passed through the narrow doorway
from death to life,
to make it wide enough for all to follow.
Nothing can ever now separate me from your love.

Lord, I Am Yours

St. Francis de Sales

Lord, I am yours,
and I must belong to no one but you.
My soul is yours,
and must live only by you.
My will is yours,
and must love only for you.
I must love you as my first cause,
since I am from you.
I must love you as my end and rest,
since I am for you.
I must love you more than my own being,
since my being subsists by you.
I must love you more than myself,
since I am all yours and all in you.
Amen.

Prayer to the Blessed Trinity

Blessed Elizabeth of the Trinity

O my God, Trinity whom I adore, help me to forget myself entirely that I may be established in you as still and as peaceful as if my soul were already in eternity. May nothing trouble my peace or make me leave you, O my Unchanging One, but may each minute carry me further into the depths of your mystery. Give peace to my soul; make it your heaven, your beloved dwelling and your resting place. May I never leave you there alone but be wholly present, my faith wholly vigilant, wholly adoring, and wholly surrendered to your creative action.

O my beloved Christ, crucified by love, I wish to be a bride for your heart; I wish to cover you with glory; I wish to love you even unto death! But I feel my weakness, and I ask you to "clothe me with yourself," to identify my soul with all the movements of your Soul, to overwhelm me, to possess me, to substitute yourself for me that my life may be but a radiance of your life. Come into me as Adorer, as Restorer, as Savior. O Eternal Word, Word of my God, I want to spend my life in listening to you, to become wholly teachable that I may learn all from you. Then, through all nights, all voids, all helplessness, I want to gaze on you always and remain in your great light. O my beloved Star, so fascinate me that I may not withdraw from your radiance.

O consuming Fire, Spirit of Love, "come upon me," and create in my soul a kind of incarnation of the Word: that I may be another humanity for him in which he can renew his whole mystery. And you, O Father, bend lovingly over your poor little creature; "cover her with your shadow," seeing in her only the "Beloved in whom you are well pleased."

The Living Flame of Love

St. John of the Cross

O lamps of fire!
in whose splendors
the deep caverns of feeling,
once obscure and blind,
now give forth, so rarely, so exquisitely,
both warmth and light to their Beloved.

How gently and lovingly
you wake in my heart,
where in secret you dwell alone;
And in your sweet breathing,
filled with good and glory
how tenderly you swell my heart with love.

Awaken Me to Your Presence

St. Mechthild of Magdeburg

O sweet and loving God,
When I stay asleep too long,
Oblivious to all your many blessings,
Then, please, wake me up,
And sing to me your joyful song.
It is a song without noise and notes.
It is a song of love beyond words,
Of faith beyond the power of human telling.
I can hear it in my soul,
When you awaken me to your presence.

Heart of My Savior

St. Alphonsus Liguori

O amiable Heart of my Savior! You are the seat of all virtues, the source of all graces, the burning furnace in which all souls are inflamed. You are the object of all God's love; you are the refuge of the afflicted and the dwelling place of the souls that love you.

O heart worthy of reigning over all hearts and of possessing the affection of all hearts! O heart that was wounded for me on the Cross by the lance of my sins, and that remains afterwards continually wounded for me on the altar in the Blessed Sacrament, but not by any other lance than that of the love you have for me!

O loving heart that loves us with such tenderness and yet is so little loved in return. Remedy such great ingratitude by inflaming our hearts with a true love for you. Would that I could go around the whole world to make known the graces, the sweetness, the treasures you give to those who truly love you!

Accept the desires I have of seeing all hearts burn with love for you. O divine heart, be my consolation in trials, my rest in labors, my comfort in anxiety, my haven from stress.

I consecrate to you my body and my soul, my heart and my life, together with all that I am. I unite all my thoughts, all my affections and all my desires to yours.

Oh! Eternal Father, I offer you the pure love of the heart of Jesus. If you reject my love, you cannot reject those of your Son who is sanctity itself. Let that supply what is lacking in me and make me pleasing in your eyes. Amen.

O Love Eternal

St. Francis de Sales

O love eternal,
my soul needs and chooses you eternally!
Ah, come Holy Spirit,
and inflame our hearts with your love!
To love—or to die!
To die—and to love!
To die to all other love
in order to live in Jesus' love,
so that we may not die eternally.
But that we may live in your eternal love.
O Savior of our souls,
we eternally sing,
"Live, Jesus! Jesus, I love!
Live, Jesus, whom I love!
Jesus, I love, Jesus who lives and reigns
forever and ever. Amen."

Come into My Heart

St. Catherine of Siena

O Holy Spirit, come into my heart;
by your power draw it to yourself, God,
and give me charity with fear.
Guard me, Christ, from every evil thought,
and so warm and enflame me again
with your most gentle love
that every suffering may seem light to me.
My holy Father and my gentle Lord,
help me in my every need.
Christ love! Christ love!

Praise and Glory

Late Have I Loved You

St. Augustine of Hippo

Late have I loved you, beauty so old and so new:
late have I loved you. And see,
you were within and I was in the external world
and sought you there, and in my unlovely state
I plunged into those lovely created things
which you made.
You were with me, and I was not with you.
The lovely things kept me far from you,
though if they did not have their existence in you,
they had no existence at all.
You called and cried out loud
and shattered my deafness.

You were radiant and resplendent,
you put to flight my blindness.
You were fragrant, and I drew in my breath
and now pant after you.
I tasted you, and I feel
but hunger and thirst for you.
You touched me, and I am set on fire
to attain the peace which is yours.

Prayer to Christ

St. Anselm of Canterbury

Lord Jesus Christ,
my Redeemer, my Mercy, and my Salvation:
I praise you and give you thanks.
They are far beneath the goodness of your gifts,
which deserve a better return of love;
but although I requite so poorly

the sweet riches of your love
which I have longed to have,
yet my soul will pay its debt
by some sort of praise and thanks,
not as I know I ought, but as I can.

Hope of my heart, strength of my soul,
help of my weakness,
by your powerful kindness complete
what in my powerless weakness I attempt.
My life, the end to which I strive,
although I have not yet attained
to love you as I ought,
still let my desire for you
be as great as my love ought to be.

The Canticle of Brother Sun

St. Francis of Assisi

Most High, all-powerful, good Lord, yours are
the praises, the glory, the honor, and all blessing.

To you alone, Most High, do they belong,
and no man is worthy to mention your name.

Praised be you, my Lord, with all your creatures,
especially Sir Brother Sun,
Who is the day and through whom you give us
light. And he is beautiful and radiant with great
splendor; and bears a likeness of you, Most High One.

Praised be you, my Lord, through Sister Moon and
the stars, in heaven you formed them clear and
precious and beautiful.

Praised be you, my Lord, through Brother Wind,
and through the air, cloudy and serene, and every
kind of weather through which you give sustenance
to your creatures.

Praised be you, my Lord, through Sister Water,
which is very useful and humble and precious and
chaste.

Praised be you, my Lord, through Brother Fire,
through whom you light the night
and he is beautiful and playful and robust and
strong.

Praised be you, my Lord, through our Sister Mother
Earth, who sustains and governs us, and who
produces varied fruits with colored flowers and
herbs.

Praised be you, my Lord, through those who give pardon for your love and bear infirmity and tribulation. Blessed are those who endure in peace for by you, Most High, they shall be crowned.

Praised be you, my Lord, through our Sister Bodily Death, from whom no living man can escape. Woe to those who die in mortal sin. Blessed are those whom death will find in your most holy will, for the second death shall do them no harm.

Praise and bless my Lord and give him thanks and serve him with great humility.

Treasures of the Spirit

St. Mary Magdalene dei Pazzi

Holy Spirit, Spirit of truth
you are the reward of the saints,
the comforter of souls,
light in the darkness,
riches to the poor,
wealth to lovers,
food for the hungry,
hospitality to wanderers.
You are the one in whom
all treasures are contained.

God of All

St. Patrick

Our God, God of all men,
God of heaven and earth, seas and rivers,
God of sun and moon, of all the stars,
God of high mountain and lowly valleys,
God over heaven, and in heaven, and under heaven.

He has a dwelling in heaven and earth and sea and
in all things that are in them.
He inspires all things, he quickens all things.
He is over all things, he supports all things.

He makes the light of the sun to shine,
he surrounds the moon and the stars,
he has made wells in the arid earth,
placed dry islands in the sea.

He has a Son co-eternal with himself
and the Holy Spirit breathes in them;
Not separate are the Father and the Son
and the Holy Spirit.

Exalted on the Cross

O God, You Are the Object of My Love

St. Francis Xavier

O God, you are the object of my love,
not for the hope of endless joys above,
nor for the fear of endless pains below,
which those who love you not must undergo.
For me and such as me, you once did bear
the ignominious cross, the nails, the spear:
A thorny crown transpierced your sacred brow;
What bloody sweats from every member flow.
Such as then was and is your love for me,
such is and shall be still my love for thee;
Your love, O Jesus, will I ever sing—
O God of love, sweet Savior, dearest King!

Prayer to Jesus on the Cross

St. Alphonsus Liguori

Lord, you said that when you were exalted on the cross, you would draw all hearts to you. By dying on the cross for us, you have already drawn to your love so many who, for your sake, have forsaken all things—their goods, their country, their relatives, and their life. Ah, draw also my poor heart, which, through your grace, now pants to love you.

O my Redeemer, that I could see myself stripped of every worldly affection, so as to forget all things, to remember only you, and to love you alone! I hope for all things from your grace. You know my inability to do any good: through the love which made you submit to so cruel a death on Calvary for my sake, I pray for you to assist me.

O death of Jesus, O love of Jesus, take possession of all my thoughts and affections, and grant that, for the future, to please you, O Jesus, may be the sole object of all my thoughts and desires. O most amiable Lord, hear my prayer, through the merits of your death. Amen

The Anima Christi of St. Elizabeth Seton

Soul of Jesus, *Sanctify me*.
Blood of Jesus, *Wash me*.
Passion of Jesus *Comfort me*.
Wounds of Jesus, *Hide me*.
Heart of Jesus, *Receive me*.
Spirit of Jesus, *Enliven me*.
Goodness of Jesus, *Pardon me*.
Beauty of Jesus, *Draw me*.

Humility of Jesus, *Humble me.*
Peace of Jesus, *Pacify me.*
Love of Jesus, *Inflame me.*
Kingdom of Jesus, *Come to me.*
Grace of Jesus, *Replenish me.*
Mercy of Jesus, *Pity me.*
Sanctity of Jesus, *Sanctify me.*
Purity of Jesus, *Purify me.*
Cross of Jesus, *Support me.*
Nails of Jesus, *Hold me.*
Mouth of Jesus, *Bless me in life, in death,*
in time and eternity.
Mouth of Jesus, *Defend me in the hour of death.*
Mouth of Jesus, *Call me to come to you.*
Mouth of Jesus, *Receive me with your saints in glory*
evermore.

Unite me to yourself, O adorable Victim.
Life-giving heavenly Bread,

feed me, sanctify me, reign in me,
transform me to yourself,
live in me; let me live in you;
let me adore you in your
life-giving Sacrament as my God,
listen to you as to my Master,
obey you as my King,
imitate you as my Model,
follow you as my Shepherd,
love you as my Father,
seek you as my Physician
who will heal all the maladies of my soul.
Be indeed my Way, Truth and Life;
Sustain me, O heavenly Manna,
through the desert of this world,
till I shall behold you unveiled in your glory.
Amen.

How Splendid the Cross

St. Theodore of Studios

How splendid the cross of Christ!
It brings life, not death;
light, not darkness;
Paradise, not its loss.
It is the wood on which
the Lord, like a great warrior,
was wounded in hands and feet and side,
but healed thereby our wounds.
A tree had destroyed us;
a tree now brought us life.

The Prayer Before the Crucifix
of San Damiano

St. Francis of Assisi

Most high,
glorious God,
enlighten the darkness of my heart
and give me, Lord,
a correct faith,
a certain hope,
a perfect charity,
sense and knowledge,
so that I may carry out
your holy and true command.

Your Will Be Done

Prayer of Abandonment

Venerable Charles de Foucauld

My Father, I abandon myself to you.
Do with me as you will.
Whatever you may do with me, I thank you.
I am prepared for anything.
I accept everything, provided your will
is fulfilled in me and in all creatures.
I ask for nothing more, my God.
I place my soul in your hands.
I give it to you, my God, with all the love of my
heart, because I love you.
And for me it is a necessity of love, this gift of
myself, this placing of myself into your hands
without reserve in boundless confidence
because you are my Father.

Morning Offering

St. Thérèse of Lisieux

O my God! I offer you
all my actions for this day
for the intentions and for the glory
of the Sacred Heart of Jesus.
I desire to sanctify every beat of my heart,
my every thought,
my simplest works,
by uniting them to its infinite merits;
and I wish to make reparation for my sins
by casting them into the furnace
of its Merciful Love.

O my God! I ask of you
for myself and for those whom I hold dear,
the grace to fulfill perfectly your holy will,

to accept for love of you
the joys and sorrows of this passing life,
so that we may one day be united together
in heaven for all eternity. Amen.

To Give and Not to Count the Cost

St. Ignatius of Loyola

O my Lord Jesus!
Teach me to be generous;
teach me to serve you as you deserve;
to give and not to count the cost;
to fight and not to heed the wounds;
to toil and not to ask for rest;
to labor, seeking no reward,
save that of knowing that I do your will.
Amen

Let Nothing Disturb You

St. Teresa of Avila

Let nothing disturb you.
Let nothing frighten you.
All things pass away:
God never changes.
Patience obtains all things.
He who has God
Finds he lacks nothing;
God alone suffices.

Be A Bright Flame Before Me

St. Columba

Be thou a bright flame before me,
Be thou a guiding star above me,
Be thou a smooth path below me,

Be thou a kindly shepherd behind me,
Today—tonight—and forever.

Take, Lord, and Receive

St. Ignatius of Loyola

Take, Lord, and receive
all my liberty, my memory,
my understanding, and my entire will,
all that I have and possess.
You have given all to me.
To you, O Lord, I return them.
All is yours.
Dispose of it wholly according to your will.
Give me your love and your grace,
For this is enough for me.

Save the Afflicted Among Us

St. Clement of Rome

We beseech thee, Master,
to be our helper and protector.
Save the afflicted among us;
have mercy on the lowly;
raise up the fallen;
appear to the needy;
heal the ungodly;
restore the wanderers of thy people;
feed the hungry;
ransom our prisoners;
raise up the sick;
comfort the fainthearted.

Prayer for Peace

Blessed Pope John XXIII

Let us pray with all fervor for the peace which our divine Redeemer came to bring us. May he banish from the souls of men whatever might endanger peace. May he transform all men into witnesses of truth, justice and brotherly love. May he illumine with his light the minds of rulers, so that, besides caring for the proper material welfare of their peoples, they may also guarantee them the fairest gift of peace.

May Christ inflame the desires of all men to break through the barriers which divide them, to strengthen the bonds of mutual love, to learn to understand one another, and to pardon those who have done them wrong. Through his power and inspiration may all peoples welcome each other to their hearts as brothers, and may the peace they long for ever flower and ever reign among them.

Index of Saints

Alphonsus Liguori (1696-1787) was born in Naples, and abandoned a brilliant legal career to become a priest. He founded the Redemptorist congregation to minister to the poor in Italy. A celebrated moral theologian, he is a Doctor of the Church.

Anselm of Canterbury (c. 1033-1109) was born in Italy, and became a monk in 1060 in Normandy. In 1092, he was named archbishop of Canterbury. A prominent theologian, he is a Doctor of the Church.

Augustine of Hippo (354-430) was born in Northern Africa, and converted to Christianity in 387. In 395, he was consecrated bishop of Hippo. He wrote prolifically on doctrine and scripture, and is a Doctor of the Church.

Bernard of Clairvaux (1090-1153) was a monk who was instrumental in the rapid spread of the Cistercian order. His famous writings include commentaries on the love of God and on the Song of Songs. He is a Doctor of the Church.

Charles de Foucald (1858-1916) led a wild, undisciplined life until he experienced a conversion and became a monk. He lived in the Sahara desert, caring for and evangelizing the people. He was killed by Muslim gunmen.

Catherine of Siena (1347-1380) was a mystic and reformer who persuaded the pope to return to Rome. Her famous *Dialogues* describe Christ as a bridge to heaven. She is a Doctor of the Church.

Clement of Rome (died c. 99) became pope in 91, and was exiled by the emperor, where he continued preaching. He died in exile.

Columba (c. 521-597) was born in Ireland. He established what eventually became a famous and influential monastery on the island of Iona, off the coast of Scotland.

Elizabeth Ann Seton (1774-1821) was a widow and the mother of five children when she converted to Catholicism. She founded the Sisters of Charity, a teaching order, based in Emmitsburg, Maryland.

Elizabeth of the Trinity (1880-1906) was born in France. She entered a Carmelite monastery in Dijon at the age of twenty-one, and died five years later.

Francis of Assisi (1181-1226) was the famous monk and founder of the Order of Friars Minor, who loved nature, poverty, and simplicity.

Francis de Sales (1567-1622) was Bishop of Geneva who, with St. Jane de Chantal, co-founded the Visitation Order. He was a much-loved spiritual director who authored the classic *Introduction to the Devout Life*.

Francis Xavier (1506-1552) was one of the founding members of the Society of Jesus and one of the first missionaries of the order. He died off the coast of China in an attempt to enter that country.

Ignatius of Loyola (1491-1556) was born in the Basque region of Spain. After being wounded in battle, he had a conversion experience and wrote his famous *Spiritual Exercises*. Together with six other men, he founded the Society of Jesus.

John of the Cross (1542-1591) was instrumental, along with St. Teresa of Avila, in reforming the Carmelite order. A great mystic, he authored some of the world's great spiritual classics.

Mary Magdalene dei Pazzi (1566-1607) was born in Florence, Italy, and entered a Carmelite convent in 1582 The descriptions of her revelations were published after her death.

Mechthild of Magdeburg (c. 1210-c. 1285) was born of a noble family in Saxony and at the age of twelve began experiencing divine inspirations. The last twelve years of her life were spent in a Cistercian monastery.

Patrick (c. 389-c. 461) was born in Britain, the son of a Roman official, and was kidnapped to pagan Ireland when he was sixteen. He later escaped, was ordained, and was sent to Ireland. There he traveled throughout the island, bringing Christianity to the entire population.

Pope John XXIII (1881-1963) grew up in a poor family in northern Italy. After ordination, he served a string of diplomatic posts throughout Europe. In 1953, he became cardinal of Venice, and in 1958, he was elected pope, and launched the Second Vatican Council.

Teresa of Avila (1515-1582) was born in Spain and entered a Carmelite convent at the age of twenty. After struggling for twenty years to develop a deeper prayer life, she began receiving mystical gifts. She is the author of many great spiritual classics on prayer, including *Interior Castle*, and is a Doctor of the Church.

Theodore of Studios (759-826) was born in Constantinople. He became a monk and was abbot of the famous Studios Monastery in that city, which became a center of Eastern monastic life. He was exiled and imprisoned several times for denouncing various actions of the emperor.

Thérèse of Lisieux (1873-1897) entered a Carmelite monastery at the age of fifteen, and died at the age of twenty-four of tuberculosis in the same monastery. Her autobiography, *Story of a Soul*, described her "little way" to God and became an instant classic. She is a Doctor of the Church.

Acknowledgments

• Prayers of St. Francis of Assisi from *Francis and Clare, The Complete Works*, translation and introduction by Regis J. Armstrong, O.F.M. Cap., and Ignatius C. Brady, O.F.M. Copyright ©1982 by the Missionary Society of St. Paul the Apostle in the State of New York. Used by permission of Paulist Press.

• Prayer by St. Catherine of Siena taken from *The Prayers of Catherine of Siena*, edited by Suzanne Noffke, O.P. Copyright ©1983 by Suzanne Noffke, O.P. Used by permission of Paulist Press.

• Prayer of St. Mary Magdalene dei Pazzi taken from *Breakfast with the Saints*, Copyright ©1996 by Servant Publications. Published by Servant Publications, Box 8617, Ann Arbor, Michigan, 48107. Used by permission of Servant Publications.

• "Heart of My Savior" by St. Alphonsus Liguori taken from *The Holy Eucharist* by St. Alphonsus Liguori, edited and abridged by Msgr. Charles Dollen, copyright ©1994 by the Society of St. Paul. Used by permission of Alba House, New York.

• Prayers of St. Patrick, Charles de Foucauld, St. Clement of Rome, St. Columba, and St. Mechthild of Magdeburg taken from *The Complete Book of Christian Prayer*. Selection, arrangement and indexing of this anthology copyright ©SPCK 1995. Used by permission of The Continuum International Publishing Group Inc.

• Prayer of St. John of the Cross from *The Collected Works of St. John of the Cross*, translated by Kieran Kavanaugh and Otilio Rodriguez. Copyright ©1979, 1991, by Washington Province of Discalced